Dear Parent:

Your child's love of reading starts here!

Every child learns to read in a different way and at his or her own speed. Some go back and forth between reading levels and read favourite books again and again. Others read through each level in order. You can help your young reader improve and become more confident by encouraging his or her own interests and abilities. From books your child reads with you to the first books he or she reads alone, there are I Can Read Books for every stage of reading:

SHARED READING
Basic language, word repetition, and whimsical illustrations, ideal for sharing with your emergent reader

BEGINNING READING
Short sentences, familiar words, and simple concepts for children eager to read on their own

READING WITH HELP
Engaging stories, longer sentences, and language play for developing readers

READING ALONE
Complex plots, challenging vocabulary, and high-interest topics for the independent reader

I Can Read Books have introduced children to the joy of reading since 1957. Featuring award-winning authors and illustrators and a fabulous cast of beloved characters, I Can Read Books set the standard for beginning readers.

A lifetime of discovery begins with the magical words **"I Can Read!"**

Visit www.icanread.ca for information
on enriching your child's reading experience.

MISTY COPELAND:
BALLET STAR

by Sarah Howden
pictures by Nick Craine

Collins

Ruby bounced in her seat.

Then she got up and did a twirl,

just like Misty Copeland would do.

She was so excited this day

had finally come!

"You're such a show off,"
said Ruby's sister, Jasmine.
"Try to get along, girls,"
Mama said.

Ruby was too happy to mind
Jasmine's teasing.

This was the best Christmas present
she had ever gotten.

Ruby had been taking ballet lessons for three years now.

Ruby had Misty Copeland's poster
on her wall.
But she had never seen
a real, live ballet.

Now Ruby was at *The Nutcracker.*

It starred Misty Copeland

as the Sugar Plum Fairy!

Ruby tapped Jasmine on the shoulder.
"Did you know Misty only started
dancing when she was thirteen?"
Ruby asked. "That's old!"

"Well, it's not exactly old,"
Mama said with a chuckle.
"But most ballet dancers start
when they're three or four."

"So Misty had to learn a lot really fast," said Ruby. "Plus her family didn't have the money for lessons."

"But Misty was so good that
her teacher taught her for free!"

"Really?" said Jasmine.

"She'd even drive Misty home
when she needed a ride," said Ruby.

"Misty didn't have it easy,"
Mama said.

"People told her that her body was
wrong for ballet."

"That's because she was so strong,"
Ruby said.

She flexed her muscles.

"But Misty proved them wrong."

Mama nodded. "Now she's the first African American principal dancer in the American Ballet Theatre!"

"That means star dancer,"
Ruby whispered.

Jasmine raised her eyebrows.

"I knew that," she said.

But Ruby knew she was impressed.

Jasmine had quit ballet years ago.

Ruby didn't understand that at all.

Just then, the lights dimmed.

The curtains opened.

The ballet was starting!

Soon Misty would appear.

The stage looked like a bright
fairy-tale world.
The dancers were like dolls.
Ruby loved to watch them
twirl and glide.

Then Misty danced onto the stage.

Misty floated along on her toes.

She leaped as if she could fly.

"She's just like a fairy,"

Ruby said.

The crowd clapped and cheered
when Misty danced.
"One day I could be up there,"
Ruby told herself.

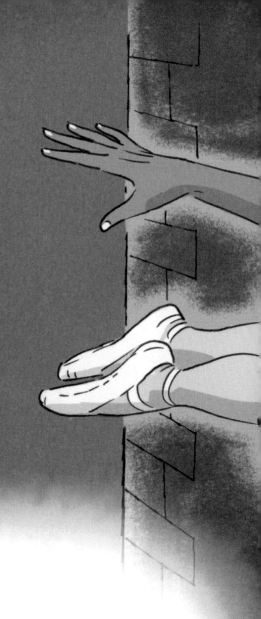

A dancer lifted Misty high into
the air and the crowd gasped.
She was so graceful, like a swan.

24

When the show ended,

the crowd was on its feet.

Ruby clapped as loud as she could.

She cheered the most for Misty.

Ruby was sad it was over.

"Let's go get a milkshake,"
Mama said.

"Misty was great," Ruby said.

"She really was," said Jasmine.

Ruby blinked.

Had Jasmine agreed with her?

"It must have been hard being the only black person in her classes," said Jasmine.

"I'm sure it was," said Mama.

"But now she has opened the door for many more people of colour," Mama said.

"Like me!" Ruby said.

Jasmine was quiet.

Then she said, "Mama, can I start taking ballet again?"

Mama smiled widely.

"Absolutely," she said.

"If Misty can do it, so can you."